Washington D. C. Mayor

Message of the Mayor of the City of Washington

Transmitted to the two Boards of the City Council, July 19, 1869

Washington D. C. Mayor

Message of the Mayor of the City of Washington
Transmitted to the two Boards of the City Council, July 19, 1869

ISBN/EAN: 9783337144319

Printed in Europe, USA, Canada, Australia, Japan

Cover: Foto ©ninafisch / pixelio.de

More available books at **www.hansebooks.com**

MESSAGE

OF

THE MAYOR

OF THE

CITY OF WASHINGTON,

Transmitted to the Two Boards of the City Council, July 19, 1869, and the

Reports of the Water Registrar, Board of Fire Commissioners, Superintendent of the Fire Alarm Telegraph, and Intendant of Washington Asylum.

———⊶◇⊷———

CHRONICLE PRINT,
WASHINGTON, D. C.

MESSAGE OF THE MAYOR.

Mayor's Office, City Hall,

Washington, D C., *July* 19, 1869.

To the Board of Aldermen and Board of Common Council:

Gentlemen: —In accordance with custom, and with the requirements of the charter of the city, I have the honor of transmitting for your consideration, the following communication relative to the condition of the city and its affairs during the fiscal year just closed, and of calling your attention to such measures as, in my opinion, requires the action of the Councils recently installed into office.

We have enjoyed a season of uninterrupted and unexampled prosperity, which has had the natural effect to increase our wealth and population, and give an impetus to improvements and business that cannot fail to be gratifying to every citizen, as well as every well-wisher of the nation's capital. In no one year have so many first-class buildings been erected, nor so many public improvements been made within the city limits as in the fiscal year just closed. This has silenced the declarations of many, that in consequence of our proximity to the great battle ground of the rebellion, and the sympathy of some of our people with the South, a clamor would be raised against retaining this as the seat of the General Government, which would result in its removal to one of the great cities of the West. Now that its permanency as the capital of the nation appears assured, it behooves us to make the most of the advantages we possess over other cities, from this as well as other causes, and to strive to keep pace with the progress and spirit of this enlightened age. To do this, much will be required of the Councils, but the results will amply repay for every sacrifice that any or all of us are called upon to make.

STREET IMPROVEMENTS.

There have been graded and graveled during the year, of the streets—

Graded and Graveled.		Graded Only.
In the First Ward, - - - - 30 squares.		60 squares.
In the Second Ward, - - - - 33 "		23 "
In the Third Ward, - - - - 6 "		0 "
In the Fourth Ward, - - - - 10 "		0 "
In the Fifth Ward, - - - - 8 "		0 "
In the Sixth Ward, - - - - - 9 "		0 "
In the Seventh Ward, . - - 8 "		46 "
Total, - - - - - - 104 "		129 "

Of sidewalks and gutters, there have been curbed, graded, and paved—

In the First Ward, - - - - - - - - - - -	51 squares.
In the Second Ward, - - - - - - - - - -	17 "
In the Third Ward, - - - - - - - . - - -	10 "
In the Fourth Ward, - - - - - - - - - -	17 "
In the Fifth Ward, - - - - - - - . - - -	26 "
In the Sixth Ward, - - - - - - - - - - -	32 "
In the Seventh Ward, - - - - - - . - - -	24 "
Total, - - - - - - -	177 "

Number of squares of streets paved in the city, 10; number of intersections paved in the city, 6.

Number of bridges erected and repaired, 13; number of alleys graded and paved, 6.

The filthy condition of the streets, gutters, and alleys at the time of the appointment of the present ward commissioners, rendered it necessary to employ a large force to cleanse and purify them, in order to prevent disease and pestilence. I doubt if ever before a city was left by an administration as a legacy to its successor in such a state as was this in the month of June, 1868, when I was inaugurated. To clean and put in respectable order was the first duty devolving on the new administration Of course, a heavy expense was necessary, but it was accomplished ; and it is a fact admitted by all, that the city, during the past year, has been kept cleaner and in a better sanitary condition than ever before. It is hoped and believed that the expense on this account, now that the *old filth* has been removed, will be comparatively, this year, much lessened.

FINANCIAL STATISTICS.

The revenues of the city for the fiscal year have been—

From ten-year bonds issued, - - - - - . - -	$387,000	00
From taxes on real and personal property to May 31, - - - - - - - - - - - - - -	570,570	64
From taxes for month of June, not reported by collector, estimated, - - - - - - -	50,000	00
From markets and licenses, - - - - - - -	162,129	03
From water taxes, - - - - - - . - - - -	49,369	67
From special taxes, redemption and surplus funds,	241,394,66	
From all other sources, - - - - - - - -	29,138	25
Total, - - - - - -	$1,489,602,28	

The expenditures have been—

For salaries of officers, - - - - - - - -	$34,119	40
For expenses of Councils, - - - - - - -	30,081	53
For Police Department, - - - - - - - -	68,354	94
For station-houses, including fuel, - - - - -	3,582	89
For schools and school-houses, including loan of previous year, with interest on the same, ($62,469,43.) - - - - - - - - - -	241,376	72
For Fire Department, - - - . - - - - -	26,263	23
For Water Department, - - - - - - - -	33,908	14
For Asylum, - - ` - - - - - - . - - -	18,961	15
For gas-lamps, repairs, and lamp-lighters, - -	22,055	53
For markets, including improvements, - - - -	10,801	91
For grading and graveling streets, - - - -	64,715	80
For flag footways, - - - - - - - - - -	37,446	17
For bridges, erection and repairs of - - - -	11,118	94
For repairs of streets, - - .- - - - - - -	31,871	72
For sewers, - - - - - - - - - - - -	3,971	91
For cleaning streets, alleys, and gutters, - - -	60,324	89

For improvement of City Hall, - - - - -   2,620 75
For interest on funded debt, - - - - - - -   59,026 92
For payment of floating debt, in bonds, - - - 387,000 00
For payment, in cash, small fractional balances
   not included above, - - - - - - - -   6,951 69
For sinking fund, ten-year bonds, - - - - -   70,565 32
For special tax, redemption and surplus funds, 234,912 00
For all other purposes, including Board of Health, 30,614 27

          Total, - - - - - - $1,490,645 82

Excess of expenditures over receipts, - - -   1,043 54
   The above includes payments in cash on indebtedness incurred by former administrations, as follows:
Indebtedness matured previous to July 1, 1868,
                      $161,287 05
Indebtedness matured since July 1, 1868, incurred by previous legislation, principally contracted for, but not matured, - - - - -   95,030 84

   Total cash payments on old liabilities,   256,317 89
   The estimated receipts for the current year, exclusive of water and special taxes and trust funds, will be—
From taxes, at ($1 40 on $100), - - - - - - $1,000 000
From markets, licenses, and all other sources, - 290,000

          Total, - - - - - -   1,290,000
   The estimated expenditures necessary to meet current expenses, and complete such improvements as are demanded by the people, are—
For salaries of officers, - - - - - - - - $36,000
For expenses of Councils, - - - - - - - -   32,000
For Police Department, including new station-
   houses, - - - - - - - - - - - -   75,000
For schools and school-houses, including new
   sites and buildings, - - - ː - - - - -   250,000
For Fire Department, including the purchase of
   two new steam fire engines, erection of
   houses, &c., - - - - - - - - - - -   50,000

For Asylum, -   .   . .   .   .   . - -   20,000
For gas-lamps, repairs, &c.,   - -   75,000
For markets, - · - · - · -   · - - ·   10,000
For grading and graveling streets, -   ·   · ·   80,000
For flag footways, - · - · - · - ·   40,000
For bridges, including three over Tiber creek, -   40,000
For repairs of streets, - · - · - · - · - ·   30,000
For sewers, including cost of reconstructing that
     on Fourteenth street, - · - · - · - ·   25,000
For cleaning streets, alleys, and gutters, - · -   60,000
For interest on funded debt, - · - · -   ·   89,000
For sinking fund, - · - · - · - · - ·   50,000
For all other expenses, - · - · -   ·   60,000

                Total,   · - · - · -   1,022,000

Leaving a balance of $268,000, which will be amply sufficient to pay all existing liabilities, and leave to the credit of the Corporation on the 30th of June, 1870, the sum of $100,000.

The rate of taxation above indicated ($1 40 on the $100) may appear somewhat high, and the sum to be raised by it more than is actually necessary. But it is less, much less, than that paid by other cities more favorably circumstanced than we now are. We need more improvements in our streets, more of which should be opened; more bridges and flag footways are imperatively demanded; more roadways must be paved, the intersections of which cost large sums of money; more sewers should and must be constructed immediately, the laterals of which, with the drops, man-holes, and traps, are a heavy tax on the ward funds. The Fourteenth street sewer requires to be relaid from end to end ; wells and pumps are clamored for all over the city; a station-house should be erected in every ward, and comfortably furnished for our policemen ; school houses built where necessary, in order to save the thousands paid for rent of inconvenient and poorly adapted school-rooms. The sea-wall on the west side of South Washington should be removed outward to the river channel, and the space filled in, so as to give place to wharves on the river front ; gas must be extended on most of the streets; the people who are without light and who pay as much for lighting other streets as they who derive the benefit of such light, clamoring and constantly complaining about it, and other extraordinary expenditures, which none but those who are required to audit and pay the bills would ever think of, are requisite, which amount to a very large sum during the year.

But these improvements more than pay the cost of construction in the enhancement of the value of real estate in the city, which comes back to the tax-payers in this way four-fold, to say nothing of the additional comfort, convenience and satisfaction they afford. Who does not know that this city (whether justly or unjustly does not change the fact) has the reputation of being a century behind others of a like population in all that relates to public improvements and progress, when, as the capital of the Republic, the resort of people of all nations, we should be foremost in these things? To effect this object, money is required, and the only way to obtain it is through taxation. Besides all this, we have thousands of mechanics and laborers unemployed, many of whose families are suffering for bread. We should strive to give these employment as far as possible to make them and their families comfortable and contented, by doing which much that tends to vice and crime will be destroyed, and the morals of the people improved. And how can this be so profitably done as by putting the idle poor, who are willing and anxious to work, but are totally unable to get it, to performing labor on the streets? The result will prove the wisdom of such a course, not only by what is above stated, but by the reduction of the number in our jail and almhouse, and a comparative reduction in the cost of maintaining those institutions, for nothing so much as idleness begets immorality and crime.

The funded debt of the city is as follows:

Certificates of 5 per cent. stock issued under act
    of August 19, 1828, - - - - - - - $54,807 00
Certificates of 6 per cent. stock issued under act
    of October 25, 1843, - - - - - - -   685,517 38
Chesapeake and Ohio canal bonds, - - - -   48,800 00

Washington and Alexandria railroad bonds, guaranteed by the city, - - - - - -	18,500	00
Water stock, - - - - . - - - - - -	155,000	00
Ten-year bonds issued under act of October 17, 1868, - - - - - - - - - - - - -	387,000	00
Total funded debt, - -	$1,349,624	38
Of the floating debt existing on the 30th of June, 1868, authorized to be paid by the ten-year bonds, a large proportion of which is in suit, the holders refusing to accept bonds, there is estimated to remain outstanding the sum of - - - - - - -	$100,000	00
And there has been paid out of the revenue of the fiscal year just closed, of the same debt, in cash, the sum of - - - - - - - -	161,287	05
Amount chiefly contracted for but not matured, July 1, 1868, paid also in cash, - - - -	95,030	84
Which, added to the amount of bonds issued, -	387,000	00
And bonds not delivered June 30, - - - -	18,650	00
With fractional balances still due, - - - -	3,418	49
Makes the total floating indebtedness existing on the 30th June, 1868, - - - - - -	$765,386	38

The amount in bank to the credit of the interest and sinking fund for the redemption of the ten-year bonds was, on the 30th of last month, $70,565 32, which is a larger sum than is necessary to be raised, the law requiring only one-tenth of the amount of the bonds issued, and the interest on the whole, to be collected in each year. The rate of taxation on this account can therefore be materially reduced the present year.

A large portion of the water stock falls due the present year, and the entire amount will soon be payable. No provision has been made by our predecessors in office for the payment of any portion of this debt, and the whole burden of it falls unjustly on us. There is now standing to the credit of the water fund the sum of $19,530 39, which is more than sufficient to pay the year's portion of the debt. The remainder will have to be provided for without delay, and I recommend that authority be given me to anticipate the revenues from the water fund to enable me to redeem the stock as it is presented.

By the report of the water registrar, transmitted herewith, it will be seen that the amount of water taxes outstanding are:

Due and payable, - - - - - - - - - -	$25,221 71
Yet to fall due, - - - - - - - - - -	58,018 38
Total, - - - - -	$83,240 09

The entire receipts of the water fund since the introduction of Potomac water, exclusive of loans, have been, as nearly as can be ascertained, - - - - - - - - - - $286,823 56
The loans have been, - - - - - - - - 173,500 00

Total, - - - - -	460,323 56

The entire expense of the distribution of water since its introduction has been, - - - - 438,583 18

Balance of receipts, including loans, over expenditures, - - - - - - - - . - - $21,740 38

Actual expenses over actual receipts, $151,759 62; deficit, if all outstanding water taxes were paid, $67,519 53.

POTOMAC WATER.

Much complaint has been made during the past few years of a deficiency in the supply of water, especially in the more elevated portions of the city. This defect arises from the fact that the water-mains leading from the reservoir to the city are not of sufficient size to allow of the flow of the necessary quantity through them. There are now two mains, and the only permanent remedy is to provide another, or more -than one, as the case may require, which will involve a large expenditure of money. I recommend that some action be taken in regard to this matter, in order that a full and ample supply of water, so necessary to the health, comfort, and convenience of our people, may be obtained. The increasing demand for the Potomac water, and the extension of water-mains to all parts of the city, thus increasing its consumption and the dependence upon it, render this a subject of vital importance.

It is with much regret that I am called, by my sense of duty to the corporation, to state to you that the late Water Registrar, although called upon on several occasions to render a statement of his account with the water fund during the last several years of his administration, has still failed to do so. And the present incumbent of the office has found it impossible to ascertain the true condition of such accounts when he entered on his duties, there being in the office no books or papers from which that information could be obtained.

In order that it may be shown to the satisfaction of the people, as well as of Congress, the exact amount that has been collected and disbursed on account of the water fund since the introduction of the Potomac water into the city, I suggest that measures be taken at once to obtain from the late Registrar a true statement of his accounts during his official term ; and in this connection I may, with propriety, refer to section 5 of the act of the Corporation of June 2, 1859, and call the attention of the Councils to the duties required of them by that act.

OFFICERS OF THE CORPORATION.

As a general rule, the officers of the Corporation have performed their duties faithfully, and with satisfaction to the people. That, with rare exceptions, all have done the best they could for the interest of the city I am fully convinced. Where such has been the case it would appear invidious to discriminate; but, as the bookkeeper and clerk to the Mayor have been under my own eye, and I have been personally cognizant of their fidelity, ability, and the very heavy labors required of them, I take the liberty to state that, in my opinion, they are inadequately paid for their services, and I therefore recommend that their salaries be increased—that of the bookkeeper to $2,000, and that of the clerk to $1,500 per annum. I very much doubt whether any other clerks in this city perform as arduous and responsible duties as they for anything like the compensation they receive.

PUBLIC SCHOOLS.

The success of our public schools and the improvements of the system of teaching and discipline are causes of congratulation. With a little more experience on the part of some of our teachers, with more of an interest in the education of their children evinced by the parents of such as attend the schools, and with the guidance of an experienced general superintendent, such as we now have, it is to be hoped that our public schools will in a very short time equal, if not excel, as they should, those of any other city in the Union. In any measure calculated to promote the efficiency of these schools, and to extend the system so that every child, white and colored, rich and poor, within our limits, shall have the benefit of a good education, you will find me ready and anxious to co-operate with you.

More school-houses are required in different sections of the city. The exorbitant rents paid for poor and ill-adapted school-rooms would soon cover the expense of erecting good, plain, substantial buildings where they are needed. I cannot too strongly commend the subject to your favorable consideration.

The total receipts on account of the school and school-house funds for the fiscal year were—

From taxes,		$156,722 16
From general fund (deficit of 1866–7)		10,907 36
Total,		$167,629 52

Expended during the same period, through Treasurer of the public schools—

For teachers' salaries,		$59,898 41
Music teachers,		1,575 00
Care of school-rooms,		3,907 36
Rent of school-rooms,		16,774 76
Fuel and stove fixtures,		6,153 64
Contingent expenses,		29,225 45
Salaries of Secretary and Treasurer,		500 00
Contingent expenses of the Board,		2,279 57
Total,		$120,314 19

Through Mayor's office—

For Franklin school-house.	-	$35,585 82
School-house in 4th district,	-	6,677 00
Incidentals,	-	512 81
Colored schools,	-	38,683 84
Loan of June 8, 1868, with interest, charged up at bank,	-	62,469 43

Total,   -   -   - $264,243 09

Of this amount was paid on previous indebtedness, in cash, $107,814 78; in bonds, $22,868 75; total, $130,683 53.

HIGH AND NORMAL SCHOOL.

The early establishment of a scientific high and normal school has become a necessity. Upon the completion of the Franklin school building, rooms for such a school could be set apart therein, to be used until the finances of the city will justify the erection of a building exclusively for the purpose. The manifest advantages resulting from such an institution lead me to hope that by the time of the opening of the public schools for the next scholastic year authority will be given to establish one on such a basis as will give to it the utmost efficiency and usefulness.

THE COLORED SCHOOLS.

The schools for colored children in this city, with some exceptions, have been maintained during the past year with a considerable degree of efficiency; but they might have attained much higher excellence and success had they been under the management of experienced and well-qualified directors. In my judgment, the time has arrived when these schools should be incorporated with our other public schools, placed under the same management, be conducted on the same system, and share impartially in all respects the same advantages. The Board of Trustees of Public Schools should consist of both white and colored members, in due proportions, and no difference should be allowed in the qualifications of teachers on account of the color of the pupils. The exigency which required the temporary creation of a separate board of trustees for colored schools has now happily passed away. It is much to be regretted that the action of Congress at its last session, providing for the termination of this separate system, should have been defeated by the veto of Andrew Johnson, through the influence and misguided efforts of a few of the very class for whose benefit it was intended.

The distinction of color is no longer recognized in our charter nor at the ballot-box, in the courts of justice, the lecture-room, the hall of public amusement, the public conveyance, nor in the City Councils. It should be eliminated as speedily as possible from our school system. The breaking down of all caste distinctions is one of the great missions of the American people, and the sooner all classes "conquer their prejudices" and accept the situation, the better for all concerned. All children should be educated as the children of American citizens, the future sovereigns of the Republic, and should be taught to ignore all class distinctions. Nowhere can this be done so effectually as in the common school, by the daily exercises of the school room, where merit and achievement only give precedence. And, on the other hand, by no method will the animosities and peculiarities of race and caste be so surely perpetuated and intensified as by the keeping up of separate systems of education in our schools.

That all right minded citizens should agree and co-operate in this important matter is eminently desirable. The character of all our schools should be, and by proper efforts might be, so elevated that no "contamination," but only the improvement of all classes would result from such association. But in view of the differences of opinion and the bitter, foolish prejudices which have existed, and to some extent still exist, it is a question how soon and how far the mingling of races in the same school can be effected without causing the withdrawal of some of those who most need education. In my judgment, this may eb safely left to the wise discretion of a board of trustees constituted as I have already suggested, and having at heart the best interests of all classes.

Experience has already shown that the difficulties in the way are not so great as many imagine. White parents of respectability and culture have urged the admission of their children into colored schools *where superior teachers have been employed*, for the sake of the higher advantages there afforded. It is believed that were all the schools placed under one board properly constituted, and were a part of the schools designated as open to both classes, care being taken to provide teachers of the highest qualifications, numbers of white as well as colored citizens would, voluntarily and as a matter of principle, place their children in such schools, at least until the experiment should be fairly tested. And it is further believed that the results would be such that, without violence, popular excitement, or the withdrawal of any considerable number of children from school, the barrier of caste would quietly melt away, and all the schools be speedily thrown open to all who need them. Then would our school system be established on the basis of a broad and impartial nationality, which knows not race nor color, but only Americans and children of a common Parent.

I therefore recommend that measures be taken to represent this matter before Congress at its next session, with a view to obtaining such action as shall place all our schools under one management, with discretionary power as to the mingling of the classes heretofore separated. This subject cannot longer be evaded, as a bill is pending in Congress, with every probability of its becoming a law, which contemplates and requires that all the schools of this District shall be open for the reception and instruction of pupils without distinction of class.

These colored schools, and the expense attending their support, have grown to a magnitude not anticipated at their beginning. The revenue at first amounted to a little over $300 per annum. Their board of trustees have been paid out of the city treasury about $40,000 the past year, and the amount will be largely increased the coming year. This is the only revenue for the support of these schools, and the corporation has no voice in their government, is not consulted in regard to the appointment of trustees or teachers, nor are the trustees accountable for their action or for the disbursement of this large sum to the Government or the Corporation. Indeed, as the case now stands, they might appropriate the money to any other use, and there is no law authorizing the city or any other power to compel them to account for it. If this separate system is to be continued, I recommend that Congress be applied to for the passage of an act requiring the trustees to enter into bond in a sufficient sum, with security satisfactory to the Mayor, for the proper application of the funds, and also requiring them to make an annual report to the city authorities, giving a detailed statement of their operations.

ASYLUM AND FIRE DEPARTMENT.

For a detailed statement of the expenses of the Asylum, and of the Fire Department, I beg leave to refer to the reports of the commissioners thereof, which are herewith transmitted.

The United States Government having withdrawn the three steam fire-engines in use here since the war, a necessity exists for supplying their places by the Corporation. Arrangements have already been made for the purchase of two engines, and I recommend that authority be given for purchasing another without delay. Proper protection to property renders this absolutely necessary. The Government having a very large amount of property here requiring protection from fire should, in common justice, pay its portion of the expense of procuring the proper engines, and maintaining a Fire Department in the city.

HOUSE OF INDUSTRY, ETC.

I ask the attention of the Councils to the necessity of establishing a house of correction and industry for juvenile offenders, and a home for the aged and friendless in our midst. No other city in the United States, so far as I know and believe, having a population so large as this, has so little accommodation for the poor and unfortunate. A school-ship moored in our river might, like those in Boston, serve to reclaim vicious and unruly boys, who, by a proper course of training and study, would become qualified for seamen on Government vessels or merchant ships, or for any other respectable occupation. It is a disgrace to our city that we have no refuge for these classes except our poor-house and jail, where they are brought in contact with hardened villains, and become as wicked as they. If the city would take the lead in this matter, and commence the erection of proper buildings, I have no doubt that Congress would, as it justly should, lend a helping hand and appropriate its share toward completing the work. Let the Councils make the experiment ; Congress will do its share if we show a determination to do what we ought for ourselves

A NEW JAIL AND A POLICE COURT.

I beg leave again to call the attention of the Councils to the absolute necessity of erecting a new jail in this District, such as is provided for in the bill now pending in Congress. Although, under the wise management of the able and efficient officer now in charge of that institution it has been brought to as high a state of perfection as can possibly be reached in such a building, still, the reasons existing at the time of my last message, one year ago, for a new structure are now in force, and I cannot too urgently recommend that the attention of Congress be early called to this subject It is a discredit to the District that we have no better place for confining persons charged with offenses, all classes of whom, without regard to age, sex, or condition, are necessarily thrown together in this worse than pest-house, there to concoct and indulge in schemes of vice and villainy, till relieved by the slow and uncertain process of our crude and unwholesome code of criminal law, most of which was enacted more than a century ago.

We also need a police court for the speedy trial of offenders. A bill is now pending in Congress establishing such a court, which would, if passed into a law, afford relief, and be productive of the happiest results. The Councils should press the importance of these matters on our national legislature, and, if possible, procure the passage of the bills referred to at the next session.

RAISING THE GRADE OF PENNSYLVANIA AVENUE.

The great difficulty of properly draining and sewering property on Pennsylvania avenue, between Ninth street west and the Capitol gate, suggests the propriety of raising the grade of

B

that avenue sufficiently above tide water in time of floods to prevent its overflow and the filling of basements and cellars with water. This would involve the holders of property and the city in a large expense; but it must be done sooner or later, and it can be accomplished now at a less cost than at any future time after the buildings and improvements to be affected by the change shall have become more valuable. And it is believed that the increased value of the property will more than cover the cost; besides, it will render the drainage and sewerage perfect by making the descent from the high ground north of the avenue to the canal regular, and prevent the bursting of sewers by reason of pressure of water through the almost level ground south of the avenue, and the "backing up" of the water from the canal into the sewers.

Of course, the authority of Congress will be required to do this work, and the Government will pay its share of the cost.

This may be regarded by some as visionary, but a full investigation of the subject will satisfy any practical person of its utility and necessity. Although the proposed change will involve a heavy expenditure of money, the advantages to be derived from it will amply compensate the property-holders and the city for the outlay. Other cities have expended millions for raising the grades of and widening streets, where the necessity was nothing compared with this; and the experiment in every case, so far as is known, has not only proved a public benefit, but has resulted in an enhancement of the value of the property affected by it more than doubly sufficient to cover the cost.

This matter is submitted for your consideration If you approve the suggestion, I recommend that application be made to Congress at the next session for authority and aid to effect the desired object.

WASHINGTON CANAL.

I have again to call the attention of the Councils to the condition of the Washington canal. The opinion I have heretofore expressed on that subject remains unchanged; but if anything better can be suggested, I am ready to assent to and approve it.

And if it be the desire of the people of the city that it shall be cleaned out and rendered navigable, and their representatives so decide, it will be necessary for them to impose a special tax of at least $300,000 on the assessable property of the city to cover the expense, the same to be provided for this year; or that sum will have to be diverted from the proposed, and, as I think, more necessary, legitimate and profitable work of opening and repairing streets. We can employ just so many laborers with the money we raise, and if *they* work on the canal others cannot be employed on the streets. So far, then, as the laborer is concerned, it certainly makes no difference with him whether the canal is ever cleaned or not, unless the people are willing to pay enough extra tax to foot the bills. Will the tax-payers assent to this? It is for the Councils to determine, but I opine they will look well to their pockets before making an investment on which they can never hope to realize a dividend or the least profit. I can never consent that this property be alienated by the Corporation and placed at the tender mercy of a private company.

The plan proposed in my last message, and more recently in effect by the late Superintendent of Sewers, &c., to arch the canal and convert it into a main sewer across the city, is doubtless the most feasible plan of disposing of this troublesome and vexatious subject; and, as the reclaimed land will more than cover the cost, I confess that I am unable to see the force of the objections urged against it. In its present condition the canal is unquestionably a festering nuisance, and I trust that some action may be taken without delay looking to an abatement of the evil. The office of Commissioner of the canal I deem unnecessary. The duties of such an officer can be performed by the Superintendent of Sewers, &c., and I recommend that authority be given him for that purpose.

RIVER AND HARBOR IMPROVEMENT.

Our river channels and harbor should at once be improved. We have on both sides of the city a sufficient depth of water to float almost any vessel. Miles of water front, which in any other city would be converted into a mine of wealth, are entirely neglected, and there is not a wharf worthy the name at which a vessel can receive or discharge a cargo. This can only be accounted for by the fact that our city, until a recent date, was cursed with an institution that 'lighted everything it touched as by fire. But that time has passed ; a new era has dawned upon us, and progress, enterprise, energy and activity should prevail in lieu of the dead past. We must keep pace with the progressive spirit of the age, or go into bankruptcy and wind up.

REMOVAL OF SEA WALL.

I recommend that measures be immediately taken to remove the sea wall on the west side of the Island to the channel, and that the space be filled in, thus reclaiming a large area of valuable ground which can be used, rented, or sold for wharf sites, and made to yield a large revenue to the city, as well as to add materially to its commerce and other business. Congress will undoubtedly aid in the improvement of our river and harbor, when we show a disposition to do what we can to effect that necessary object. This aid has been given in the States. Is it not unjust to withhold it here where Congress has exclusive jurisdiction?

ADVERTISING THE TAX LIST.

A great cause of complaint with our tax payers who are not fortunate enough to have the means of paying their taxes when due, is the heavy cost of advertising and sale. As this profits neither the lot-holder nor the Corporation, but goes to enrich others having no claim on either, I suggest that the law be so changed as to avoid it as far as possible. The wisdom of the Councils will enable them to devise some method to abate this great evil, and save our property holders from such an imposition.

In the meantime, the very large amount of taxes uncollected calls for some action that will compel such as are able to pay and will not, to discharge their liabilities on this account promptly.

There are on the books of the Collector's office general taxes uncollected, as follows :

Prior to 1866, running back to 1843. - - - - $25,167 90
For the year 1866, -   - - - - - - -   6,186 36
For the year 1867, - - -   - - - - -   - - - 15,658 70
For the year 1868,   - -   - - - - - -   60,695 22

Total uncollected, - - - $107,708 18

The impossibility of collecting these taxes, owing to the reluctance of persons to purchase property at tax sales, suggests the necessity of providing for the enforcement of tax collections as far as possible, promptly each year. This great and growing evil calls loudly for legislative action by Congress. But, as a means of present relief existing within the powers of the Corporation, and as an inducement to property holders to pay their taxes without delay, I recommend that in the tax bill for the present year there be inserted a clause authorizing and requiring the Collector to add to each bill a certain rate per cent. a month on all sums remaining unpaid after the first day of September or October next. Such a measure has proved salutary where it has been tried, and it is believed will induce tax payers here to settle up as soon as possible

MARKET HOUSE.

Your attention is called to the necessity of erecting another market house in lieu of the present Centre Market. The plan proposed in the bill introduced by Senator Harlan, at the last session of Congress, appears to give very general satisfaction, and is undoubtedly the most feasible of any yet suggested. I recommend, therefore, that efforts be made to induce Congress to pass said bill which will give the necessary authority for erecting a building on the site named, and another on the reservation between Tenth and Twelfth streets, near the canal, for the sale of coarse articles and live stock, that will be a credit to the city and a source of very large revenue. Indeed, it is believed that the rents alone would be sufficient to pay the expense of the building in five years, including the expenses of attendance and repairs.

PARKING THE AVENUES AND STREETS.

The great width of our streets and avenues renders it proper, in order to save the useless expense of keeping them clean and in proper traveling condition, that a portion of them be parked. Various plans have been suggested but it appears to me that it would be the wisest and cheapest method to remove the curb-stone on each side, say from ten to twenty feet, according to the width of the street, into the carriageway, and make a grass-plat with a row of trees in the centre of the space, between the foot pavement and the curb. This will not only save the expense of paving, cleaning, and repairing so much of the street, but will add greatly to the health, beauty, and comfort of the city. The experiment once tried, on a single street or square, I am certain it would be universally adopted. Before making this alteration, however, and especially before paving any roadway, I would advise that a sewer, with water and gas-mains, be laid on each side of the street near the outer line of the footwalk, in order to save the necessity of opening the street into the centre at any time when the sewer or water or gas-mains require to be tapped; or the pipes leading therefrom to be repaired. This laying two sewers and mains might cost a trifle more at first than one twice as large in the middle of the street, but it would be more eco-nomical in the end, as much less service-pipe would be required, and not half the amount of excavation. Besides, the annoy-ance of cutting through the roadway and ruining streets and pavements would be entirely avoided.

PAVING LOUISIANA AND INDIANA AVENUES, ETC.

The avenues leading to the City Hall (I refer to Louisiana and Indiana avenues) should be paved at once. Their condition in the winter renders them dangerous for travel, and it is a source of great annoyance to our people, as well as a discredit to the city, that these great thoroughfares should remain longer unim-proved.

North Capitol street should also be opened from the Capitol grounds to G street, from which it has been well graded and graveled, to the northern boundary of the city. This is the street leading directly from the Capitol to the Government Printing Office, and, if opened and put in good traveling condition, will be used by the teams almost constantly running between those points, instead of their going around by New Jersey avenue, as is now done. It being a great convenience and a saving of expense, therefore, to the Government, Congress, I am satisfied, will willingly reimburse the Corporation, a portion if not all of the cost of opening this street.

BALTIMORE AND OHIO RAILROAD.

The only difficulty in the way of making North Capitol street one of the handsomest leading from the Capitol is its constant obstruction by the Baltimore and Ohio Railroad Company, which uses that street as a convenient depot for unemployed freight and passenger cars, makes up trains and keeps them standing on the street for any length of time, and thus prevents its use, as well as the use of the streets crossing it, by teams or otherwise. This is all in clear violation of the charter of the company, which forbids that it shall interfere with the free use of the streets on which the road runs or over which it crosses ; but it entirely disregards the law, and treats the Corporation and the interests of private individuals with contempt. It assumes to control the grades of our streets ; and when the Corporation proceeds to execute its laws and ordinances for grading such streets and laying the footwalk thereon, it is met with resistance and a spirit of defiance that might lead to the supposition that the Baltimore and Ohio Railroad Company, and not Congress and the Corporation, is sovereign over Washington. If the position taken by that company, that the present bed of their road is to govern the grades of the streets, is to be acceded to, the Corporation had better abandon the idea of ever improving that portion of the city which the road traverses, and hand over to the company absolute and final jurisdiction, if not the fee simple in the land, for every one knows that the streets cannot be opened on that grade, nor can the streets or sidewalks crossing the road ever be used or drained. But I have no idea that Congress or the Corporation will yield to its insolent demands, nor that our courts will sustain it in its absolute pretensions. I am well aware that it has become purse-proud and overbearing, that it boasts its power to bring the Corpora tion to the foot of the throne of its haughty president, that it refuses to pay its quota of taxes for the support of the city government; but we shall see whether right or might will triumph in the capital of the nation—whether the monopoly that undertook to break up the Government at the opening of the rebellion, and afterwards grew fat and pompous on its extortions from the Government when it had failed in its purpose, shall remain sovereign here, or yield a little to some other power.

The following bill shows the amount of taxes unpaid by the Baltimore and Ohio Railroad Company, as reported by the Collector:

Baltimore and Ohio Railroad Company to Washington Corporation, Dr.

Tax on property for 1855,	$296 32
Tax for 1856,	320 40
Tax for 1857,	370 37
Tax for 1858,	370 37
Tax for 1859,	156 26
Tax for 1860,	711 38
Tax for 1861,	555 56
Tax for 1862,	2,133 22
Tax for 1863,	2,127 86
Tax for 1864,	3,071 39
Tax for 1865,	3,337 67
Tax for 1866,	3,671 42
Tax for 1867,	4,172 09
Tax for 1868,	5,006 50
Erecting pump in square 888,	12 06
	$26,312 87

These taxes were levied on the following described property :

Square.	Lot.	Value of Lot.	Improvements.
718	all.	$11,995	$1,600
831	of 1	198	
	" 2	103	
857	" 2	2	
	" 3	49	
	" 4	99	
	" 5	153	
	" 6	175	
	" 7	170	
	" 8	306	
	" 9	4	
	" 15	4	
	" 16	56	
	" 17	85	
	" 18	156	
	" 19	192	
887	" 1	36	
888	" 6	200	
	" 7	1	
632	all.	78,183	60,000
		$92,167	$61,600

Total value of lots,	. . . . .	$92,167 00
Improvements,	. . . .	61,600 00
Rolling stock,	. . . .	80,000 00
Railroad stock,	. .	100,000 00
Grand total,	. . . .	$333,767 00

For this sum of $26,312 87, which has been accruing for fifteen years, and which the Corporation has been totally unable to collect from the company, I have instructed the Corporation Attorney to bring suit in our courts.

REGULATIONS NECESSARY TO PREVENT ACCIDENTS.

I cannot too strongly recommend the Councils to invoke authority from Congress giving the Corporation full power to
compel all railroads running into the city to conform the same
to the legal grade of the streets, and, in order to avoid accidents,
I also recommend that the railroad companies be required to
restrict the speed of trains within the city limits to four miles
an hour, and to station a flagman or signal officer at the intersection of their road with each graded street of the city, to give
notice of the approach of trains. Also, that an ordinance be
passed imposing heavy penalties on any company for obstruct-
ing any street, by suffering trains or cars to remain on it when
not in motion.

IMPROVEMENT OF THE AVENUES BY THE GENERAL GOVERNMENT.

Pennsylvania avenue, the great thoroughfare of the city, is in
a wretched condition, and requires to be newly paved with
wood or some other approved material. The other avenues
(all of which are under the jurisdiction of Congress) should,
to keep pace with the opening of the streets by the Corporation,
be graded and graveled, or paved and placed in good traveling
condition. This is but an act of justice to the city, as the fail-
ure to grade these avenues, in many cases, renders it impossible
for the city to open and grade the streets required for travel.
It is believed, now that the executive and legislative departments
of the Government are in accord with the authorities of the city,
that an application to Congress by the Councils to have this
work accomplished will be successful, and that Congress, if
properly applied to, and the facts are fully laid before it, will
deal liberally with the city in regard to public schools, the
improvement of certain streets in the vicinity of public property,
the construction of sewers, &c. For these things we have a
right to expect appropriations, as it is the duty of the Government to pay the expense. In asking it, therefore, we are but
applying for our rights, and should not be regarded as *beggars*.

LIGHTING CERTAIN STREETS AND AVENUES.

The recent act of Congress requiring the city to light Pennsylvania avenue, as well as othes avenues and streets hertofore

lighted at the expense of the United States, with gas, is viewed by all our citizens as unjust and oppressive. So long as Congress asserts jurisdiction and control over these avenues and streets, and the Government uses them as much as or more than our own people, it ought to have them lighted at its own expense, or at least to share with the city the cost of lighting This is but an act of simple justice, and will not be denied if properly and fairly represented.

GOVERNMENT AID FOR SCHOOLS.

Nor will it be denied that a handsome donation is due from Congress to aid in sustaining our public schools. Here Congress has exclusive jurisdiction, and although there are thousands of children to be educated in this city whose parents have been brought here by the Government and the exigencies of the rebellion, who are not in reality citizens here, owning no property, and paying no taxes into the city treasury, still not a dollar has ever been given by Congress for schools, while land and money have been lavished on the States and Territories for educational purposes, to aid them in educating *their* children. This is all wrong, and with proper efforts on the part of the Councils, I hazard nothing in stating that Congress will "make haste" to correct the injustice complained of.

DISBURSING OFFICER.

I recommend that a disbursing officer be designated to pay the laborers on the streets, in the markets, &c. The impropriety of paying these persons through the hands of those by whom they are employed is too manifest to require an explanation. The ward commissioners, clerks of markets, and others employing men, should be required to furnish to such disbursing officer monthly rolls of their employees, verified by oath as to their correctness, and payments should be made in accordance therewith. Such a course will secure to each laborer his proper wages, and take from the persons who employ men on Corporation work every inducement to make improper returns, and will save the Corporation, in my opinion, a large sum of money. Besides, it will prove more satisfactory to our citizens.

28

PAY FOR LABOR AND MATERIALS FURNISHED CONTRACTORS

If the contract system is to continue, duty to the laboring men of the city, as well as to those who furnish materials, requires that I should call your attention to the fact that some of the contractors have, within the past year, after drawing the amounts due them from the Corporation, failed to pay the men who did their work, and those who supplied them with materials. This should be guarded against as much as possible, and I recommend the passage of a law authorizing the Register to retain from the assessments in each case a sum sufficient to satisfy all claims of the character mentioned, that shall be furnished him with satisfactory evidence of their correctness, until such claims are satisfied, or to pay the same to the claimants themselves after a specified period of time has elapsed, and the contractor still refuses or fails to satisfy them. This would save the officers of the Corporation much annoyance and trouble from this class of men, who entertain the idea, to some extent, that the city is bound to see them paid, and clamor month after month for their money, when in reality the contractor is the only party to whom they can legally look for their dues. But should not the Corporation, so far as it is in its power, protect these people from loss through designing contractors?

SCAVENGERS AND NIGHT SOIL.

I have on several occasions called the attention of the Councils to the great difficulties under which the scavengers of the city perform their labor. The point has been reached at last when their operations must cease or legislation must afford them relief. The plan of deodorizing the night soil, which can be done at a trifling expense, appears the most feasible; but the whole subject requires investigation and intelligent action, and I trust it will not be overlooked or postponed.

STREET RAILROADS.

Your attention is called to the condition of the street railroads, neither of which complies with the requirements of its charter in relation to keeping the spaces between the rails and tracks, and for two feet outside the rails, paved and in proper condition. This is an evil requiring speedy and prompt action Incorporated companies having valuable franchises within the limits of the city should be made to comply with the laws giving them a corporate existence, or to surrender the privileges granted them that they may revert to the Corporation

RAILROAD COMMUNICATIONS WITH WASHINGTON.

The want of railroads communicating with the city, north, south, east and west, has long been felt, and the subject has been so thoroughly discussed and is so well understood by all that it would be superfluous in me to attempt to add anything to awaken an interest in its importance. I will therefore content myself with the statement that, in my opinion, it will be necessary for this Corporation, unless it is willing that all the channels of trade, commerce, manufactures and material wealth shall be forever closed against it and diverted to rival cities ; unless we are satisfied to lie idle and suffer the tide of progress and prosperity, ready to flow in upon us, to recede ; unless we wish to have renewed the agitation of the subject of the removal of the capital of the nation to some more enterprising city of the far West ; we *must* be up and doing, and provide for more cheap and more accommodating means of travel and freight to and from this city. We cannot, therefore, do better than to turn our attention to this subject, and endeavor to obtain from Congress authority to subscribe to the capital stock of such railroads as are in contemplation or course of construction communicating with this city, or to issue bonds to a proper amount to aid in their completion. No other investment could be made that would yield such profitable returns.

MANUFACTURING CAPITAL NEEDED.

With additional railroads freights will be cheapened, the cost of provisions and raw materials lessened, and manufactures such as our almost unequaled water-power invites would soon follow, and with them an era of improvement and progress hitherto unknown. We should not be satisfied to let the future growth of our city depend merely on the fact that it is the nation's capital, and that the Government supports a large population by the payment of large salaries to its officials located here. We have other and more important resources, and it is our plain duty to cause them to be developed. This done, the threat too often made of a removal of the seat of the government of the United States need have no terrors for any of us.

CARE NECESSARY IN LEGISLATION AUTHORIZING IMPROVEMENTS.

I cannot too strongly urge upon the Councils the necessity of great care in passing bills calling for appropriations of money from the city treasury. Bills of this character authorizing improvements to be made often embarrass the Executive of the city, who is compelled by the importunities of parties interested to order the work to be done, and thus to involve an expenditure not perhaps absolutely necessary. Nor should any work be authorized involving an expense beyond the original appropriation, to fix the amount of which a careful estimate should be required of the city official under whose supervision the work is to be done. The practice of requiring the Mayor to contract for grading and graveling streets at a price per yard, and appropriating a few hundred dollars therefor, when it will require more than as many thousands to pay for it, cannot be too strongly condemned. It is impossible for any one to estimate the expense of the Corporation from year to year so long as it continues.

CONCLUSION.

During the past year our city has been wonderfully favored, for which we have abundant cause to render thanks to that Divine Power that watches over and controls all things for the benefit of His creatures. We have been blessed with health. Peace and prosperity have abounded. No calamities by fire or flood have overtaken us. Crimes of great and less magnitude have been few compared with other cities similarly circumstanced, and law, order, and propriety have generally been observed by all classes of our people. Intemperance, that bane of many who would otherwise be ornaments to society and useful to the world, is largely on the decrease, and it is now a rare circumstance that an intoxicated person is seen in the street. Reforms are general, and, unless something intervenes to stop their progress, we will soon be more free from vices incident to large cities than any other city in the Union. The many calamities that were to befal us in case of emancipation and universal suffrage have proved mere phantoms of the brains of disordered and *unprofitable* prophets, whose wish was undoubtedly "father to the thought."

The comparatively insignificant though unfortunate disturbance which took place in the Second Ward in this city on the occasion of the recent municipal election, would be deemed unworthy of mention as an exception to these remarks, were it not for the extravagant exaggerations in relation thereto which have been circulated throughout the country for political effect, and to the detriment of the fair fame of this capital. It is well known in the community where this disorder occurred that it was provoked by acts of the most offensive and exasperating character on the part of a single individual who had before rendered himself personally obnoxious to numbers of his fellow-citizens by dishonest practices. The violence, therefore, while it was without justification and is deeply to be regretted, had far more of personal than of political significance, and it was happily suppressed without loss of life or of property.

The masses of our people are becoming more and more enlightened and moral. Old prejudices and animosities, engendered by the slave system, are disappearing. Free schools will soon be open to all, and every child in our midst, who will, may have the benefits of a good education.

Within the past year the people have placed in the executive chair of the nation the great soldier who conquered a peace and brought traitors to a realizing sense of what it is to make war on the Government; and only one month ago the people of this city again proved their capacity for self government, their ability to vote and act intelligently, by electing the friends of freedom, the friends of equal rights in all that pertains to manhood and the elevation and progress of the human race, to legislate for and rule over them and the city, by majorities as unexpected as they were decided and significant What may we not reasonably expect to result from a combination of favors and circumstances such as are here related ?

For blessings such as these should we not be thankful ? And while we render thanks for the past, let us prove ourselves worthy of future blessings by making use of those faculties with which Providence has endowed us to improve our own and the condition of our fellow man ; to develop the resources placed within our reach ; to keep pace with the onward and upward march of the age, and to render our beautiful city what it was designed by its exalted and beloved founder to be, worthy the American people, and worthy of being known and honored as the capital of the greatest, the freest, and the most enlightened nation on the face of the earth.

The foreg ing are my individual opinions and views on the various matters to which they relate. They are communicated to you for your consideration and action. If they meet with your favor and regard I shall be gratified ; if not, and the Councils agree to reject them and substitute those of their own, it will be my aim and purpose to co-operate with them and carry out the will of the majority. I am ready to submit to any sacrifice of opinion in order to secure harmony between the different departments, and to maintain the best interests of the city.

Invoking the aid of Almighty God in your deliberations and action, and His continued blessing on our beloved city, I trust that our counsels may be so guided as to effect the greatest good to the greatest number, both to ourselves and our posterity.

Very respectfully, your obedient servant,

S. J. Bowen, *Mayor.*

REPORT OF THE WATER REGISTRAR.

OFFICE OF WATER REGISTRAR, CITY HALL,
WASHINGTON, D. C., *July* 2, 1869.

Hon. Sayles J. Bowen, Mayor:

SIR :—I have the honor to submit the following report for transmission to the Boards of the City Council :

The last annual report made by my predecessor in office, so far as I have been able to ascertain, was dated March 1, 1864, and hence I am not afforded such data, and such a continuous exhibition of the condition of our water distribution and of the transactions of this office up to the date of my accession thereto, as would render an annual report at this time a simple statement of the business of the office for the past fiscal year. Without, therefore, any report of last year as a basis, I shall aim to make a general statement of the transactions of the office for the year ending on the 30th *ultimo*, together with such facts and suggestions as may possibly be of interest to yourself, the Councils, and the public, and afford some information which may be useful in framing future legislation for the government and improvement of the Water Department. An ordinance of the Corporation contemplates an annual report from the Water Registrar in January; but to accord with our general system, and in consideration of the fact that I had then been in office but a fraction of a year, I have deemed it more essential that it should embrace the fiscal year, and have acted accordingly.

I entered upon my duties as Water Registrar on the 11th of July last, without the privilege of such introduction to its varied duties as is customary from an outgoing to an incoming public officer—but soon familiarized myself with the work to be done. There were no books in the office showing the condition of the Water Fund or of the accounts of the retiring officer, and none have since been received. This is a matter, however, which belongs to the Councils rather than myself; but if records

c

had been kept as a part of the system of the office showing the amount of receipts from each source of its revenue, they would be very valuable for preservation and
reference, and would have rendered unnecessary much
of the labor which I have had in preparing some of the
statistics of this report.

When I entered upon the duties of this office it was
an active part of the year in respect of making new water
connections, making up the assessment of water tax
for a portion of the mains laid in 1867, collecting the
water tax, of which one instalment falls due annually
in July, and preparing to lay new mains, while a large
number of water rents for 1868 remained to be collected,
repairs to be made, &c.

WATER RENTS.

The whole number of water rents at the present date,
with a general classification, and the annual value of the
rents of each class, is shown by the following table, as
made up from the books of the office ; but this is not a
correct criterion of the actual receipts from this source,
for the reason that in some cases the water has been
taken for only a part of the year ; in others it has been,
for various reasons, temporarily discontinued, while in a
few instances it is still due and unpaid.

Classification of Rents.	Number.	Value.
Private Dwellings,	4,052	$19,676 70
Hotels, Restaurants, and Bars,	174	2,628 00
Stores, Banks, &c.,	122	639 00
Gas Holders,	3	200 00
Engines (Locomotive,)	9	800 00
Engines (Stationary,)	22	411 00
Stables,	72	665 75
Breweries,	12	333 15
Barber Shops and Public Baths,	16	183 00
Bakeries and Confectionaries,	16	57 00
Miscellaneous,	17	193 50
Churches, Public Schools, and Chari-table Institutions, for which there is no charge,	92	
Total,	4,607	$25,787 10

On the 31st of December, 1863, the last date to which I find any similar report. the whole number of water-takers was 2,098, and the value of the water rents $14.-822 75, showing an increase in the past five and a half years of 2,509 in the number of places supplied with Potomac water, and of $10,964 35 in the annual value of the rents. In this statement the public buildings and other establishments belonging to, or occupied by, the General Government are not taken into the account.

The number of places supplied with Potomac water for the first time during the year ending on the 30th ult., is 809, and that number of taps has consequently been made by the Inspector and Tapper of Water Mains.

The amount actually collected for water rents during the past fiscal year is $25,110 51. Of this sum $2,442 66 is for rents of 1868, and of which $2,277 41 was collected by me; $22,667 85 is for rents of 1869, making the total amount of water rents collected by me during the fiscal year $24,945 26.

In this connection I would say that, by the munificent provision made by the General Government for supplying this city with water, our citizens are afforded one great convenience and necessity at a much lower rate than is paid therefor in other places; and by a comparison of our water rates with those of the other principal cities of the country I find that they are, on an average, not more than one-fifth as high. In no city have the officers of the water department been less inquisitorial in examining as to the use of water or allowed a more liberal consumption without extra charge. This leniency is often abused by an extravagant use and waste of water, which the growing shortness of our supply requires should be remedied. Our basis of assessing water rents is. for domestic use, the number of stories and front width of the house supplied, which, after a careful examination of the systems adopted in other cities, I am satisfied is best adapted to our circumstances. Were our rates higher, it would be well to take into account the number of rooms in each house, and also to make a separate charge for street washer, water closet, bath tub, &c : but without increasing our general rates these items are too small to compensate for the extra labor and expense of their assessment and collection. For hotels and other establishments requiring a large supply of water, the use of water meters would, in my opinion, be a very great improvement, and probably save a very large quantity of water which is so much needed for ordinary domestic purposes in the more elevated parts of the city. The use of meters is increasing in other cities, and I would recommend their adoption for hotels, breweries, steam engines, gas works, stables, and similar establishments, which now pay a fixed water rent, generally inadequate and often but loosely proportioned to the amount of water used. Both by preventing waste and by an increase of revenue would the city be repaid for the cost of the meters, varying from $20 to $40 each, should authority be given for their purchase and adoption. The imperfection of such meters has retarded their coming into general use, but late improvements have been achieved which render them both accurate and practicable.

WATER TAXES.

A tax of seven-eighths of one cent per square foot is assessed upon all property binding upon a street where a water main is laid, to reimburse the expense of laying the same, which is payable in five annual instalments, or in one payment, with a discount of six *per cent.*, at the option of the owner of the property. The amount of this tax collected during the past fiscal year is $28,361 10. The whole amount collected since the same was first assessed in 1865, as I have made the compilation from the thousands of margins of receipts given therefor, is $143,-624 78. The amount of such tax assessed and remaining unpaid, as obtained by a somewhat laborious process, with the proportion which was over-due prior to the 1st instant, and that which falls due the present month, and on the 1st of July in the subsequent years, is shown by the following table, as also the different years in which the same was assessed. The taxes of 1865 and 1866 are included under one head, as they both draw interest from the same date.

Table showing amount of outstanding Water Tax, &c.

Date of Assessment.	Over-due June 30, 1869.	Not due June 30, 1869.
Taxes of 1865 and 1866,	$19,204 72	$27,578 82
Accrued Interest,	3,450 84	4,964 18
Tax of 1867,	761 28	2,762 81
Accrued Interest,	91 34	331 53
Tax of 1868,	1,610 88	8,835 91
Accrued Interest,	96 65	570 15
Tax of 1869.		12,974 98
Total,	$25,221 71	$58,018 38

The taxes for 1865–6 were assessed, under an act of Congress, upon all mains laid prior to that date, while subsequently the tax has been assessed only upon the mains laid each year; hence the large amount for those years compared with the others. It is part of my experience to be frequently asked by persons coming to pay this water tax, why, since the General Government built the Aqueduct, and the owners of property pay this tax for laying the mains, any rent for the use of the water should be necessary.

These inquiries are answered by considering,

First. That this tax is payable in five annual instalments, so that unless it is voluntarily paid sooner, but *one-fifth* of the cost of the mains is available to the water fund to offset the disbursements of each year, even supposing the above-named rate of assessment to cover the expense, which is frequently not the case, owing to the great width of our streets and the large amount of property belonging to the General Government and not liable to the tax.

Second. That almost constant, and sometimes heavy, expenditures are necessary to repair leakages in the mains and prevent the damage to streets, sewers, and other public and private property, which would be a disastrous consequence of neglect in this particular.

Third. That soon after the organization of the Water Department, ten years ago, a loan of $155,000 was deemed necessary in order to extend the circulation of water from the few main arteries provided by the General Government, by laying new water mains, prior to the authorization of this tax, and water stock was issued for that amount, upon which the interest has been regularly paid, but to meet the principal of which, to fall due as hereinafter stated, no surplus or sinking fund has accumulated from the revenues of this office; and

Fourth. That the fire hydrants, of the most approved and efficient pattern now in use, have been erected along the lines of the water mains to the number of about five hundred, which, as safeguards against the destruction of property, certainly enhance its value in a ratio far exceeding their cost.

Thus it becomes necssary to supply this defficiency, for the time being, in the tax intended to cover the expense of laying the mains, (four-ñfths of it being in deferred payments), as well as to defray the expense of repairs and fire hydrants, above-named, and what source at once so appropriate, just and equitable as a moderate charge for the use of water?

REPAIRS.

During the year repairs of some eighty leakages in mains, stops and fire hydrants have been made, new stop-boxes have been put in at the street crossings whereever rendered necessary by the decay of the old ones, some thirty stops have been paved around, to the great improvement of the streets and increased safety of travel. At the Centre market, on my accession to office, the fire hydrants, being of the old pattern, were in a leaky condition, and while they were of little or no service in the important respect of cleansing the market and protecting it from fire, they were very active agents in the waste of water.

These hydrants were replaced by others, and those in the Northern Liberty market have been repaired, and one in the Western market. All this work under the head of "Repairs" has been done by the Inspector and

Tapper of Water Mains, under my direction, who has employed men for that purpose, from time to time, instead of ordering it done by plumbers or contractors, as has heretofore generally been the case.

I am satisfied that the result has been, owing in no small degree to the thorough competency of the Inspector and Tapper of Mains and his devotion to his duties, a great saving of expense, as well as the giving work to poor men who greatly need it. As an example, the price paid heretofore for paving around stops, by contract, has been $10 each, while the paving of the thirty above-named cost but $3 each, the necessary stones being procured from the Ward Commissioners without expense to the city. All the stops at the intersection of streets should be paved, as otherwise the tops or plates are knocked off by vehicles and openings left which are dangerous and might involve the Corporation in suits for damages. The expense is properly chargeable to the appropriation for "Incidental Expenses of Laying Water Mains," which should be made large enough for the purpose, or a special appropriation made therefor.

By the grading of K street, some 150 feet of water pipe laid by the War Department to the Deaf and Dumb Asylum was left above ground. This was relaid and the expense charged to the appropriation for "Repairs," as was that of resetting stop-boxes and fire-plugs, which was rendered necessary by grading or the change of grades.

LAYING OF WATER MAINS.

During the past season, after my accession to office, some 15,000 feet of 6-inch water mains were procured and laid in such localities as seemed, after a careful examination of the whole ground and a collation of the numerous acts authorizing the laying of water mains, most urgently to need them, regard being had to a fair distribution of the same to the different parts of the city, the number of houses that would be thereby accommodated and protection which would be afforded against fire in localities otherwise very much exposed. This was all the pipe which the limited resources of the water fund and the appropriation therefor would allow, although it was very far from meeting the demand. It is proposed to lay about 20,000 feet of 6-inch mains during the present season, and the work is now in progress.

Fire-plugs were erected along all the lines of the new mains, so that protection to property is made to keep pace with the convenience of a supply of water. During last fall twenty-three fire-plugs were erected, in addition to those placed in the Centre market, the expense of which was paid out of the water fund, though chargeable, under an act of the Corporation, to the several Ward funds.

A water main was laid last fall by the Freedmen's Bureau from the intersection of East Capitol and east Third streets to its tenement houses, seventy-six in number, erected in square number 1,054, extending from east Third street along East Capitol street to east Eleventh street, thence along east Eleventh to north B street, along north B to Tennessee avenue, thence along Tennessee avenue to north C street, thence along north C to east Fifteenth street, with branches along east and west sides of the square. This is a 6-inch main as far as east Fourteenth street, and the balance is 4-inch, making 6,793 feet of the former, and 1,275 of the latter size. It was laid in anticipation of its future purchase by the Corporation, and was therefore done under the general supervision of this office, and in accordance with its regulations for laying mains.

The subject was presented to the late Councils in a communication of his honor, the Mayor, and the proper Committee has been furnished with the necessary data for its adjustment..

There is a large number of 4-inch water mains in different parts of the city, which were laid during the war by the Quartermaster's Department, but which are no longer required for its use. Brevet Brigadier General J. C. McFerran, Deputy Quartermaster General, has transmitted me a list of these mains and proposed their purchase by the city at an appraised valuation to be made by a person acting on behalf of his Department and one acting on behalf of the city. Some of these mains would be of good service, and as they can doubtless be purchased for a small sum compared with their cost, and most of them be put to some use, the proposition is worthy of consideration by the appropriate committees of the Councils. The main on Eighth street west, extending from N street to Boundary, is one of those included in the list above-named, and his honor, the Mayor, united with me in recommending to the late Councils its purchase at the appraised value of twenty-five cents per foot, but an act which passed one of the Boards for that purpose failed to pass the other, which I much regret, especially as, by the permission of the Quartermaster General, we had tapped the main in several instances, and our citizens are enjoying the benefits of it. Its purchase would be a great saving of expense and afford an adequate supply of water to residents along its line for many years to come, if not always. The reason why the act for its purchase did not pass would seem to be the hope that Congress would donate it to the city, but there are other and greater matters in which we may ask Congressional aid, and if we expect help in those we should show a willingness to help ourselves, at least in smaller ones.

RECEIPTS AND EXPENSES.

The receipts of this office for the year ending June 30, 1869, which have been deposited in the designated bank, were as follows:

Receipts from water taxes, - - - - -	$28,361 02
" " " rents, - - - . -	24,945 26
" " taps and permits, - - - -	2,395 00
	$55,701 28
Water taxes collected by A. G. Hall, Collector, and deposited to credit of water fund, - - - - - - - -	290 23
Total receipts of water fund, - -	$55,991 51

The expenses have been, including every debt contracted, as follows:

For Water Mains and Fire Plugs, - - -	$17,478 66
Laying Mains, - - - - - - - -	2,468 24

Interest on Water Stock, (one year's interest on $155,000,) - - - -	9,300	00
Salaries, - - - - - - - - - - -	5,821	66
Repair of Water Mains, - - - - -	1,427	00
Incidental expenses of laying Water Mains, - - - - - - - - -	706	90
Contingent expenses, including stationery, printing, keeping horse, repair of office, &c., - - - - - - -	868	53
Water Wagon, (special appropriation) -	247	00
Total, - - -	$38,317	99
Balance, receipts over expenses, - -	17,673	52
	$55,991	51

If to the above balance be added the balance to the credit of the Water Fund June 30, 1868, namely, $4,066 86, it will increase the balance to the credit of this fund on June 30, 1869, to $21.740 38. Any variance between this and the exhibit of the City Register will be owing to the fact that his statement and that of the bank are necessarily made up at an earlier date, while this statement purports to give an exhibit of the condition of the Water Fund without reference to the balancing of books, and contains some items still outstanding. The appropriations made by the late Councils, which were of specific sums, out of the Water Fund, were as follows :

For Salaries, - - - - - - - - - -	$6,255	00
Repair of Water Mains, &c., - - -	2,000	00
Incidental expenses of laying Water Mains, - - - - - - - - -	2,000	00
Contingent expenses, - - - - - -	2,000	00
Purchase of Water Wagon, - - - -	250	00

I therefore have the satisfaction of stating that the several items of expense, as shown above, fall far below the amounts appropriated. For the year ending June 30, 1868, with the same amounts appropriated, the expenses were as follows :

For Salaries, - - - - - - - - - -	$6,508	00
Repair of Water Mains, - - - -	2,719	20

Incidental expenses of laying Water
    Mains, - - - - - - - - - 4,675 13
    Contingent expenses, - - - - - 311 96

The total expenditures of the Water Fund for that year having been $56,905 62, against $38,317 99, for the year just closed. To the above balance of receipts over expenses for the past year may properly be added the amount chargeable to the Ward Funds, for the erection of Fire Plugs, and which is really due from them to the Water Funds, namely, $1,870. This would increase the balance of the past year to $19,543 52, and the present balance to $23,610 38.

This statement would present the Water Fund in a false light, were it not borne in mind that loans have been made, from time to time, for the use of the Water Department, first, by virtue of an act of Congress authorizing the issue of 6 per cent. Water Stock to an amount not exceeding $150,000, and, second, by virtue of an act of the Councils approved September 7, 1865, authorizing the Mayor "to anticipate the revenue of the Water Fund to the amount of $30,000, for the purpose of purchasing pipe, to be laid during the ensuing year."

The amount of Water Stock issued and loans made during the several years, as made up from the different reports of the City Register, is as follows :

For the year ending June 30, 1860, - - . $72,000
  "   "   "   "   "   " 1861, - - - - 32,000
  "   "   "   "   "   " 1863, - - - 15,000
  "   "   "   "   "   " 1864, - - - - 34,500
Loan for the year ending June 30, 1866, as
    per act of Councils, - - - - - - - 20,000

                Total, - - - - $173,500

There is a discrepancy between the City Register's report for the year ending June 30, 1864, and the Water Stock Books, the latter showing the issue of $36,000 of stock during that year, instead of $34,500, as given above, and the interest is paid each year out of the Water Fund on $155,000 of Water Stock, viz. $9,300, proving the error to have been in the Register's report, which has been continued through subsequent exhibits of the Water Fund. There are no books in this office, showing the receipts and disbursements of the Water Fund heretofore, but as collated from the reports of the City Register for the several years, they have been as follows :

The actual receipts of the Water Fund to June 30, 1869, exclusive of loans, $286,823 56; actual expenditures to same date, $438,583 18. Balance of expenditures over actual receipts, $151,759 62. The loans amount to $173,500, which makes the total receipts from all sources $459,323 56, and giving the balance, as hereinbefore stated, of $20,740 38. Were the outstanding Water Taxes all paid there would remain a balance of expenditures over receipts, exclusive of loans, of $67,-519 53, and a balance of receipts, *including* loans, over expenditures, of $103,980 09. The aWter Stock runs ten years from date of issue, and falls due as follows :

During the year ending June 30, 1870, - $72,000 00
"   "   "   "   "   " 1871, - 32,000 00
"   "   "   "   "   " 1873, - 15,000 00
"   "   "   "   "   " 1874, - 36,000 00

This debt cannot be regarded in the light of a blessing, whatever may be the fact in regard to the national one, and although, with proper authority, it can doubtless be renewed, yet its payment at as early a day as practicable should be aimed at, thus to relieve the at er Fund of the annual interest, which is no small draught upon its resources.

The ater Rents are constantly and steadily increasing, and with a careful husbanding of resources, an annual balance can, in my opinion, be saved and appropriated to the extinguishment of this debt, on the basis of no extraordinary expenditures being called for within the next few years.

SUPPLY AND CONSUMPTION OF WATER.

The increasing consumption, and inadequate supply of water, however, present a serious subject for the consideration of the Councils. The source of our supply at the Great Falls of the Potomac is equal to all future possibilities, but the two mains from the reservoir to the city are taxed to supply the consumption, which is enormous in proportion to our population; and the small size, and, in some instances, the almost isolation, of the mains extending long distances from the larger feeders, occasions great complaint from those residing in the more elevated and more remote portions of the city, by reason of the water being nearly exhausted before reaching such localities. This is especially the case during the principal part of the day in midsummer, when the drain is at its maximum, it being only at night and early morning that these remoter and more elevated points are afforded their necessary supply. The average daily consumption of water in this city and Georgetown for the past year was over 12,000,000 gallons, a quantity which would appear far in excess of the requirements of our population, although the consumption at the Navy Yard and for other purposes of the Government is very great. Estimating the population of the two cities at 150,000, this gives 80 gallons as the average daily consumption of every man, woman and child, while much less than one-half of that quantity is the allowance usually made in calculations relating to aqueducts and water distribution.

When it is further considered that wells are quite extensively used, and that the whole number of places using aqueduct water in this city, aside from Government buildings, is but 4,607, the consumption, compared with that of other large cities, would seem incomprehensible, except upon the theory that people waste without stint that which is furnished so cheaply and without measurement.

Take, for illustration, the following named cities:

Cincinnati, population about 250,000; average daily consumption of water for the past year, 7,623,325 gallons; Water Rents collected $334,804 82.

Chicago, population about 252,000; average daily consumption of water for the year ending March 31, 1868, 11,560,730 gallons; Water Rents collected $337,371 77.

Boston, population 230,000; average daily consumption of water for the year ending April 30, 1868, was

13,565,000 gallons. with 28,104 establishments supplied, and the Water Rents collected amounted to $550,000

Detroit, population 75,000; average daily comsumption of water for last year, 4,565,877 gallons, with 11,544 families supplied and 155 stationary engines; Water Rents collected $106,399 14.

To remedy our defective supply several plansare available, and

First. I would mention the feasibility of so limiting the waste and excessive use by the adoption of meters as hereinbefore suggested, by placing the public hydrants, which are so often out of order and the cause of immense waste, under the charge of this office, and by a rigid enforcement of the laws and regulations upon the subject of the use and waste of water, that our present supply shall be adequate to all present legitimate demands.

Second. Should an increased supply still be required, a new main from the reservoir, extending through the northern part of the city, would afford a supply limited only by the size of the main laid. The expense of such a main would be large, but if the city should take determined action in the matter the co-operation of Congress might reasonably be hoped for.

Third. A less expensive remedy would be to build a reservoir on Meridian Hill, or in that vicinity, and fill the same during the night from a main connected with the 30 inch main on K street by an engine and pump located near the Boundary. This would give back a supply through the day, and thus afford the needy relief; and, possibly it might be desirable, hereafter, to supply suburban residences in that region therefrom.

QUALITY OF THE AQUEDUCT WATER.

During portions of the year the water is not as clear as is desirable. The chief cause of this is the incomplete condition of the Washington Aqueduct. The distributing reservoir, covering an area of forty-four acres, situated near "Drovers' Rest," became in such a damaged condition in November last, by reason of the washing away of its embankments, that the water was drawn off, and it has not since been used, and probably will not be

until an appropriation shall be made by Congress to line
its banks with masonry. This reservoir was intended to
afford an opportunity for the water to settle before entering the mains; and the consequence of its disuse has
been that the water, coming more directly from the Potomac, without filtration or the chance to settle, has been
muddy when the Potomac has been swollen by rains;
and the receiving reservoir, being the natural receptacle
of a large amount of surface drainage, is not likely to be
clearer than the river itself, and at the present time,
while certain repairs are being made the water passes
through *no* reservoir, so that while this Aqueduct is a
blessing hardly to be over-estimated, yet its completion
is "a consummation devoutly to be wished."

I have the honor to be, very respectfully,

Your obedient servant,

S. R. BOND,

Water Registrar.

REPORT OF THE FIRE COMMISSIONERS.

OFFICE OF FIRE COMMISSIONERS OF THE CITY OF
WASHINGTON.

WASHINGTON, July 1st. 1869.

*To the Honorable Board of Aldermen and Board of
Common Council of Washington City:*

GENTLEMEN:—It affords us much pleasure to submit
to your honorable bodies the Fifth Annual Report of
the Washington City Fire Department, containing a
carefully prepared statement of the financial operations
of this Board, together with the reports of the Chief Engineer, and Superintendent of the Fire Alarm Telegraph, inventory of property, list of fires and alarms, list
of members of the department, and a list of stations of
the fire alarm telegraph.

When we entered upon the discharge of our duties,

we found three of the companies disorganized, the houses in need of repairs, and refurnishing ; several horses unserviceable, and the treasury empty, besides a large floating debt, and a disposition on the part of many of our citizens not to credit us.

This state of affairs necessitated a large expenditure, more than will probably be required during the coming year, as all of the engines are now in thorough repair, and our stock in good condition ; and we believe the department to be more effective than at any previous stage of its existence.

Our losses by fire have been very small, compared with those of previous years.

Your honorable bodies, having authorized the purchase and equipment of two new steam fire engines, we have taken the preliminary steps towards securing them, and trust that we shall soon be able to have them in operation.

We recommend the sale of the Franklin engine house, No. 2, and the removal of the engine to some point north of Pennsylvania avenue, as the house will soon require extensive repairs, and its removal would, in our opinion, add greatly to the effectiveness of the department. Arrangements should be made for the removal of the Columbia engine house, No. 3, as the Government will soon require the ground on which it now stands. Also that a sufficient amount be appropriated to build an engine house in the southern section of the city.

The Board would ask that two hundred copies of their report be printed for the use of the department.

Respectfully submitted.

GEO. W. GOODALL,
WM. H. GORBUTT,
JNO. H. JOHNSON,
CHARLES KING,
Board of Fire Commissioners.

E. L. CORBIN.
Acting Secretary.

Expenses of the Washington City Fire Department for the year ending June 30, 1869.

Repairs to engines, &c.	$2,885 19
Fuel	534 55
Feed...........	2,882 69
Gas..........	1,378 80
Horse Shoeing.....	182 25
Miscellaneous	6,820 78
Total expenses............	14,684 26

Appropriations and Disbursements.

Nov. 9, 1868.	Amount appropriated for compensation to the Chief Engineer and employees of the Fire Department, for the fiscal year ending June 30th, 1869.....	$16,700 00	
	Expended for that purpose....	16,700 00	
Nov. 9, 1868.	Amount appropriated for compensation of Superintendent and employees of Fire Alarm Telegraph-......	3,500 00	
	Amount expended for that purpose.........	3,500 00	
Nov. 9, 1868.	Amount appropriated for contingent expenses of Fire Alarm Telegraph............	1,400 00	
	Amount expended............	1,397 27	
	Balance unexpended.............		$2 73
Nov. 9, 1868.	Amount appropriated for the contingent expenses of Fire Department for the fiscal year ending June 30, 1869...	7,000 00	
March 19, 1869.	Additional amount appropriated for the same purpose...	1,700 00	
	Total amount appropriated....		8,700 00
	Bills paid during the fiscal year............	6,391 53	
	Amount of defalcation of W. H. Stewart, late secretary...	292 84	
			6,684 37

D

Balance now on hand...............		2,015 63
Bills remaining unpaid.		8,292 73
Leaving a deficiency of.:........		6,277 10

March 19, 1869. Amount appropriated for defi-- ciency in the appropriation for contingent expenses of the year ending June 30th, 1868......... .... — 1,800 00

March 8, 1869. Amount appropriated for entertainment of visiting firemen...... .... — 950 00

Expended for that purpose.... — 950 00

Bills remaining unpaid......... — — 766 50

Leaving a deficiency of......... — — 766 50

June 1, 1868. Amount appropriated to purchase Columbia, No. 3, engine house, unexpended.... — 500 00

May 24, 1869. Amount appropriated for purchase of new engine, &c., not yet expended.............. — 5,000 00

June 10, 1869. Amount appropriated for purchase of new engine, &c., not yet expended.............. — 5,000 00 — 10,500 00

Indebtedness prior to June 30, 1868, paid this year.

Of indebtedness existing prior to June 30, 1868, there has been paid during the current year in *bonds*............... $4,270 53

There has been paid during the present year in *cash*...... 2,319 79

Total amount paid in *cash* and *bonds*......... .... $6,590 32

General Summary.

Total amount expended for salaries for the year ending June 30, 1869............... .... $20,200 00

Total amount of contingent
expenses for the year ending June 30, 1869, including
defalcation of W. H. Stew-
art, late Secretary............ ...... 14,977 10

Total amount of expenses of
the Fire Department for the
year ending June 30, 1869,
not including the bills, &c.,
made prior to June 30,
1868, and settled during the
present year......... .... 35,177 10

Total amount of bills, salaries,
&c., that accrued prior to
June 30, 1868, but were
paid during the year ending
June 30, 1869........... .... 6,590 32

Total expense of entertaining
the visiting firemen on the
4th of March, 1869............. 1,716 50

Total expenditure of the Fire
Department for the year
ending June 30, 1869, in-
cluding the bills contracted
prior to June 30, 1868, and
paid during the present
year......... .... 43,483 92

WASHINGTON, D. C., July 1, 1869.

To the Honorable Mayor, Boards of Aldermen and Common Council of the City of Washington:

GENTLEMEN :—I have the honor to submit to you my annual report for the fiscal year ending June 30th, 1869.

As you are doubtless well aware, I assumed control of the affairs of the Fire Department one year ago, under the most disadvantageous circumstances possible. The Department came into my hands completely disorganized, as to its members, and in utter disorder as to its property.

Immediately upon the announcement of my appointment as Chief Engineer, the members of Engine Companies Nos. 1 and 2, and Hook and Ladder Company, No. 1, being bitterly opposed to me on political grounds, resigned and left the engine houses in a body, thus leaving me to begin my duties without a single man (so far as the companies spoken of were concerned) to work the apparatus or care for the stock left in the houses. One solitary company (Columbia, No. 3) remained at their post, where they still remain; and I am happy to state that I have ever found them prompt, reliable and faithful in the performance of every duty, and I feel that too much praise cannot be bestowed upon them for their good conduct in this particular. Had a fire of any magnitude occurred just at that time the result might have proved disastrous to some of the property holders of our city. In addition to this I found the engine houses dismantled to a great degree (nearly everything portable having been carried off by the outgoing companies) and purposely put in the worst condition possible. The bath tubs and water closets were in a plight which precluded all possibility of their being used in their then condition; and upon examination I discovered that the escape pipes had been stopped up by ramming down them soda water bottles, cotton waste, old shoes, etc., etc., and it was with no little labor and expense that they were put in repair and rendered fit for use. No. 1 engine was found to have been filled with stones and gravel (either by accident or design) to such a degree as to make it necessary to take it apart and cleanse it before it was deemed safe to put it into service. With this exception, the apparatus was found to be in tolerably good condition, with the exception of one hose carriage which it was found necessary to repair before putting into service.

Two of the horses at No. 1 engine house I found to be not only out of service but unserviceable, and a third suffering severely from disease of the kidneys.

I was considerably astonished on taking charge of the property of the Department to find a great discrepency between the statements contained in the inventories accompanying the last annual report of the outgoing Chief Engineer and the actual facts in the case. The last report of the late Chief Engineer was made on the 1st of July, and I took charge of the affairs of the Department on the 9th of the same month. To my surprise, I discovered that very many of the articles entered in the inventories attached to his report as on hand (among other articles, a large quantity of feed, a lot of coal, combs, brushes, &c., &c.,) were not to be found : and of the other articles which were inventoried as on hand, without any intimation of their being unserviceable, a very large majority—I should think at least two-thirds—were badly out of repair and the greater portion of them totally unfit for use. The furniture in all the houses, except No. 1, was in bad condition, being much worn and dilapidated. Many of the articles were beyond repair and had to be replaced with new. The mattresses, sheets, pillow cases and blankets were unfit for use, and it was found necessary to re-furnish all the houses, save one, with these articles.

This is the condition in which the Department was found when it came into my hands, and I immediately took measures to thoroughly reorganize it and put it in good working order. My first step was, of course, to re-fill the companies left vacant by the resignations before spoken of ; and it is hardly necessary to narrate to you here with what bitter opposition and open animosity I was met at every step of my endeavors. Suffice it to say that in a very short space of time, I had reorganized those companies, placing in them as members persons whom I believe to be quite as reliable, prompt and efficient, as any who went before them ; and it is with sincere pleasure that I now report to you that the whole Department is in excellent working order. The houses are well furnished and comfortable ; the stock is in fine condition and the apparatus in thorough repair : and the men under my control are prompt, energetic, efficient and willing, and I think I may safely say that the Department has never been more effective than now.

Appended, will be found an inventory of the property in the several engine houses, together with a detailed statement of the fires, alarms, losses, insurance, &c., as far as it was possible for me to ascertain them.

Before closing this report, I desire to use it as a medium through which to return my sincere thanks to the Mayor, Board of Fire Commissioners, and their efficient Secretary, for their unvarying kindness and courtesy towards me, and the valuable support they have so willingly extended to me in my labors during the past year: also to the officers of the Fire Alarm Telegraph, and to the Metropolitan Police force who have kindly rendered me every assistance in their power.

I desire also to thank and compliment the men who have served under me since the beginning of my term of office. In the arduous labor they have taken upon themselves—leading lives at all times fraught with danger—they have at all times performed their several duties to my entire satisfaction.

Respectfully submitted,

W. D. ELWOOD,
Chief Engineer.

OFFICERS AND MEMBERS OF THE FIRE DEPARTMENT.

George W. Goodall, Charles King, John H. Johnson, William H. Gorbutt—*Fire Commisssioners.*

W. D. Elwood—*Chief Engineer.*

E. L. Corbin—*Acting Secretary.*

J. H. Larcombe—*Superintendent Fire Alarm Telegraph.*

H. H. Bishop, H. R. Miles—*Operators.*

STEAM ENGINE COMPANY, No. 1.

C. T. Elwood—*Foreman.*

I. H. Hurdle—*Engineer.*

John S. Brent—*Fireman.*

J. W. Edmonson—*Hostler.*

H. C. Hensley, G. E. Ward, T. E. Venable, W. D. Buckley, C. Hayden, J. F. Bright—*Extramen.*

C. Day, W. Fister, F. Fugitt, W. Rowland, G. Edwards, J. V. McGraw, J. C. McConnell—*Supernumeraries*.

Steam Engine Company, No. 2.

John Dickerson—*Foreman*.

Martin Cronin—*Engineer*.

George S. Langley—*Fireman*.

R. T. Johnson—*Hostler*.

Thomas Stone, F. H. Myers, Charles Gottenkieng, John E. Piggott, John Johnson, Levi Moulding—*Extramen*.

John C. Cary, R. Williams, E. Grinnel, Lemuel Wheeden, R. Lincoln—*Supernumeraries*.

Steam Engine Company, No. 3.

James Lowe—*Foreman*.

Daniel Barron—*Engineer*.

Jasper A. Smith—*Fireman*.

M. Kane—*Hostler*.

C. Kaufman, Frank Lewis, John Gedney, Frank Fry, Walter Cox, Charles Meads—*Extramen*.

S. C. Wailes, George Jeffers, James Hess, John Kane, James Frazier, E. B. Gatton—*Supernumeraries*.

Hook and Ladder Company, No. 1.

Julius Strobel—*Foreman*.

G. N. Nicholson—*Tillerman*.

R. J. McElroy—*Hostler*.
W. Nicholson, John Dawson, R. W. Waters, James

Elwood, William S. Crew, William Anderson—*Extra-men.*

Joseph Lewis, James Jones, George Palant, P. Malone, Arthur McNally, George Mulloy, T. Hourihan—*Supernumeraries.*

OFFICE OF THE FIRE ALARM TELEGRAPH,

WASHINGTON, June 30th, 1869.

To the Honorable Mayor, Boards of Aldermen and Common Council of the City of Washington:

GENTLEMEN :—I herewith submit my annual report of the operations of the Fire Alarm Telegraph for the year ending June 30, 1869, together with such recommendations and suggestions as in my judgment the interests of the city demand, to which I invite your attention.

Notwithstanding the bad condition in which I found the telegraph at the commencement of the year, the lines and the office requiring a large amount of repairs, as well as the renovation of the office, together with the fact that it was found necessary to change the locks upon the alarm boxes and fit new keys to them, the expenses will be found to compare favorably with those of former years, and to fall considerably below the sum appropriated by you for that purpose, which was based upon the experience of previous years.

The following synopsis will be found to include all money expended, under its appropriate head :

Rent,	$250 00
Fuel and light,	313 94
Repairs of telegraph,	352 55
Battery expenses,	195 62
Incidentals,	46 77
Office and office furniture,	122 64
New keys for alarm boxes,	115 75
Total,	$1,397 27

I desire to submit to you the following estimate of expenses for the ensuing year :

Rent, - - - - - - -	$250 00
Fuel and light, - - - - - -	300 00
Repairs of telegraph, - - - - -	600 00
Battery expenses, - - - - -	300 00
Incidentals, - - - - - -	150 00
Total, - - - -	**$1,600 00**

Allow me to call your attention to the fact that for the last few years the city has been rapidly extending its limits, and that large districts, containing valuable property, have not in them a single alarm box.

I would name as localities where boxes are urgently needed the following :

At or near 20th street west and E street north.
   16th " " " P " "
   9th " " " Q " "
   New Jersey ave. " P " "
   Maryland ave. " F " "
   East Capitol st. " 12th " east.

Others might be added, but these may suffice for the present.

Another matter demands your attention, viz : The citizens are growing restive under the use of their roofs as a support for the wires, which causes leaks and injures seriously their property, entailing expenses upon the city, which are rapidly increasing, and will in the end cost far more than it will now to alter the wires. Peremptory demands have been made in many cases for their removal.

There is still another matter to which I feel that I must allude, although I do it under protest to my own feelings. The law, as it now stands, provides for the appointment of one Superintendent and two operators for the Fire Alarm Telegraph. No city in the Union having a Fire Alarm Telegraph has less than three operators, many of them four, and *they all have* in addition to these three or four operators a man for repairs.

I was tauntingly asked by a former Fire Commissioner of this city, "You did not think that you would have to do your own repairing, I guess?" Such, however, is the case. It is impossible to pick up, at the moment when needed, a man who can intelligently perform even the plainest work required, and, of necessity, the Superintendent must himself do it, or it must remain undone; and, in addition to this, owing to the scarcity of operators, he is forced to take on himself the night duty in the office.

While upon this subject, let me pursue it a step further. I informed you above that no city had less than three operators and a repair man; let me add that their salaries are in almost all the cities respectively, superintendent, $2,000; operators, $1,500; and repair man, $800 to $1,000; and this is about the compensation to men of corresponding qualifications in the commercial telegraph offices in all the cities of the country. I need offer no comment, but simply ask you to note these facts, and follow the promptings of your judgment.

Allow me, in this connection, to bear testimony to the efficiency and faithfulness of the operators who have cordially and earnestly assisted me in every emergency.

There have been, during the year, 109 alarms of fire, of which 22 were false and 3 were test alarms; 84 being from fires. many of which were so insignificant that they might be added, the list of false. The large number of purely false alarms should receive your attention, in order that such legislation may be had as will lead to the detection and punishment of the authors.

I remain yours,

J. H. LARCOMBE,
Superintendent.

REPORT OF THE INTENDANT OF THE WASHINGTON ASYLUM.

WASHINGTON ASYLUM, *June* 24, 1869.
To the Hon. Sayles J. Bowen,
Mayor, Washington, D. C.:

SIR :—In compliance with your request, I have the honor to transmit herewith statement of the expenditures of the Washington Asylum for the present fiscal year, amounting in the aggregate to $19,710 70.

I would respectfully call your attention to the fact that the expenditures of the last fiscal year, under the late administration, amounted, I believe, to upwards of $36,000, while this year the institution has been maintained on a little over one-half that amount ; notwithstanding which, I can safely declare without fear of contradiction that the inmates have been as well, if not better, fed and clothed, and are as happy and comfortable and under better discipline than they have ever been heretofore.

On entering upon the discharge of my duties here, I was fully determined to manage the institution upon the principles of honesty and economy ; and it is well known that in the beginning I was surrounded with difficulties which appeared almost insurmountable. I found neither money nor provisions on hand, and the institution was so deeply in debt that its credit was almost gone. Furthermore, every department was under the immediate control of irresponsible persons, who were not only extravagant, but, in many instances, appropriated and sold for their own special use and benefit the provisions issued in bulk for distribution to the inmates. Moreover, there were no books to show either what had been purchased or issued, and I found that the reports presented weekly to the Board of Commissioners were so grossly incorrect that some forty-three (43) inmates were reported present over and above what were actually in the institution.

Under these circumstances, my first duty was to find out how many people were actually under my charge, and the exact amount of provisions required for their consumption : to dismiss those whom I had reason to believe were engaged in pilfering and stealing ; and, while holding all to a strict accountability, to exercise a personal supervision over every department, and see that every article purchased for and issued to the inmates was put to its legitimate use, and that nothing was stolen or wasted, either in the almshouse or in the apartments of the Intendant.

In proof of the fact that I have succeeded in my endeavors to reorganize the institution, I, certainly with some degree of pride, refer to the figures showing the expenses of the past and current fiscal years, and with the thorough knowledge I now possess of the institution and its inmates, together with the prospect of a considerable reduction in the price of provisions, I feel assured that I can still further reduce the expenses during the ensuing year.

About $300, expenses of the small-pox hospital, will have to be deducted from the aggregate here presented, as that hospital has been maintained during the past year out of the appropriation for the Asylum. In this connection I would respectfully call your attention to the fact that, in the last published report of the Board of Commissioners, which was for the fiscal year ending June 30, 1867, the small-pox hospital is charged with an expenditure of nearly $7,000 ; while I am informed that the actual expenses of the hospital for that year (exclusive of the salary of the attendant, which is paid from the general fund,) amounted to considerably less than $1,000.

I am, sir, very respectfully,
Your obedient servant,
Jos. S. Martin.

Expenditures of the Washington Asylum during the fiscal year 1868-9, *ending June* 30.

FIRST QUARTER.	AMOUNT.
S. B. Wait	$322 00
Ridenour & Barr	586 92

Ridenour & Barr.. ..	537	61
Ridenour & Barr	539	50
R. Eichhorn	311	62
J s. J. Carroll	932	02
R. Cohen	978	70
Kneessi & Norfleet	66	00
J. H. Garges	70	40
Geo. W. Goodall	55	65
Geo. W. Goodall.	54	85
J. W. Selby & Co	779	36
Franklin Engine Company, (horse,)	150	00
T. T. Fowler	397	15
T. T. Fowler	831	38

SECOND QUARTER.

Ridenour & Barr	544	89
Dr. Eliot	35	00
Browning & Middleton	533	98
John Soden	50	00
Browning & Middleton..	700	67
National Republican	8	75
Kneessi & Norfleet	2	50
N. Brewer & Co.	268	48
R. Cohen	27	50
Joseph Carroll	980	57
J. H. Garges	34	57
L. Martin	67	12
H. I Gregory	79	42
Dr. Sears	329	86
R. Eichhorn	223	81
Sarah A. P. Martin.	90	00
John Sodens	25	00
John Grant.	120	00
Julius Wallace	125	00
James Welch	10	00
D. F. Atkins	200	00
Dr. Sears	849	95

THIRD QUARTER.

Browning & Middleton	521	97
Browning & Middleton	578	15
Sarah A. P. Martin	45	00
Washington and Georgetown Coal Company	140	00
Browning & Middleton	445	66
Jos. J. Carroll	881	55
N. Brewer & Co	172	35
W. L. Sears..	409	33

Browning & Middleton......	690	85
Jno. A. Baker.........	60	03
L. Martin............	42	19
L. Martin......	8	36
David Atkins......	129	00
*Michl. McClure......	25	00
*Thos. Carr......	5	00
*Jno. Craig......... .... ·	35	80
*Henry Monroe......	12	05
*Walter Smith......	3	00
Wm. A. Carroll......	50	00
John Grant......	60	00
Henry Monroe......	40	00
Anthony Gray......	25	00
R. Eichhorn......	109	17
H. I. Gregory......	12	15

FOURTH QUARTER.

Browning & Middleton......	460	57
Jno. O. Evans......	40	56
G. W. Goodall......	32	90
L. Martin.........	32	15
R. Cohen......	38	75
Approximating amount of bills becoming due this quarter	2,527	93
Total......	**$19,645**	**66**

*Paid to Jos. S. Martin.

Recapitulation of expenditures, fiscal year 1868–9.

EXPENDITURES.

First quarter......	$6 613	16
Second quarter......	5,307	02
Third quarter......	4,592	62
Fourth quarter......	3,132	86
Total......	**$19,645**	**66**

RECEIPTS.

Amount deposited with the First National Bank......	$12,067 98		
Drawn by checks......	11,863 03		
Cash in bank......	204 95		
		12,067	98
Paid by checks of Mayor Bowen......		4,253	97
Remaining unpaid		3,323	71
		$19,645	**66**

Purchases for Washington Asylum during the fiscal year ending June 30, 1869.

DATE.	NAME.	ARTICLE PURCHASED.	PRICE.
1869.			
1st, 2d, 3d, and 4th quarters......	Jos. J. Carroll	Beef, &c., per contract	$3,677 66
do. do.	R. Eichborn	Bacon and ham, do.	868 41
July, Aug., Sept., and Oct., '68	Ridenour & Barr	Groceries, &c	2,190 92
2nd, 3d, and 4th quarters	Browning & Middleton	do. do.	4,481 85
1st, 2d, 3d, and 4th quarters	W. Leslie Sears	Drugs and medicines, (contract).	1,769 19
July, 1868	S. B. Waite	do. do.	504 60
do. do.	T. T. Fowler	Coal and wood, (contract).	1,314 53
Sept., '68, and June, '69	J. W. Selby & Co.	Dry goods, &c	980 89
do. do.	R. Cohen	Blankets and boots and shoes	1,016 45
2d, 3d, and 4th quarters	Brewer & Bro.	Meal and feed.	478 49
July, '68, to June, '69.	G. W. Goodall	Plumbers' work and tinware.	143 40
do. do.	H. I. Gregory.	Stoves, pipe, tinware, &c	91 52
Sept., '68, to June, '69	Luther Martin, O	Oil, &c	149 73
May, '69	Jno. A. Baker	Garden seeds	67 03
August 31	Kneessi & Norfleet	Harness, &c	68 50
1st, 2d, 3d, and 4th quarters.	Garges Bro.	Blacksmithing	181 90
Oct. 20, '68	Johnson Eliot, M D	Consultation fee	35 20
September, '68	Chas. H. Wilson	One horse	150 00
July 31, '68	National Republican	Advertising	8 75
......	Jno. O. Evans & Co	Lumber	40 55
November 7, '68	Werner Koch	Check-book	15 00
......	Gardener, overseers, matron, &c ...	Salaries	1,431 19
......	......	Iron door	45 00
			$19,710 57

Receipts and expenditures of the Intendant Washington Asylum, in the fiscal year ending June 30, 1869.

Dr.		Cr.	
1869.		1869.	
To cash received for vegetables, fiscal year ending June 30, 1869	$1,449 49	By cash expended for marketing, fiscal year ending June 30, 1869	$961 43
To cash received for house fees and releasements	888 51	By bills paid, as per vouchers	1,495 28
To cash received for hogs, geese, board, &c	413 25	By cash paid for conveyance of hogs, geese, &c	238 75
	$2,751 25	By amount due Commissioners	55 79
To balance due Commissioners	$55 79		$2,751 25

Note.—The above is balanced to June 20, 1869.

www.ingramcontent.com/pod-product-compliance
Lightning Source LLC
Chambersburg PA
CBHW021523090426
42739CB00007B/758